Manifesting

Techniques Of Advanced Manifestation To Help You
Shift Into Your Dream Reality And Attract Abundance

*(Using The Law Of Attraction, This Is A Daily Guided
Journal That Can Help You Manifest Your Dreams)*

Tamas Schmidt

TABLE OF CONTENT

Simply Put, What Does It Mean To Heal Through Energy? 1

Filmmaking In The Mind 10

Maintain A Relationship With The Person Of Christ 16

Every One Of Us Is Interconnected 27

Have Faith In The Law Of Attraction's (Loa) Power, And Don't Be Afraid To Dream Big 37

Set Goals 42

Medicreation 47

How To Get More Energy To Meet Your Needs 54

Things Which Get In The Way Of Your Manifestation 63

What You Feel Is What You Are. 68

Be Specific Regarding Your Goals, And Make Sure The Universe Is Aware Of Them 79

Never Give In: "Never Give Up" 83

Rescue From The Wrath Of Sin 93

Manifesting Calls For Creative Thought And Action 96

Why Positive Thinking Is Effective 107

The Hidden Truth Behind The Principle Of Attraction 112

Gratitude-Centered Mentality 118

What Exactly Does "Intentional Living" Entail? 124

Bringing My Wellness Into Manifestation 139

A Simulated Scenario 145

Mastering The Art Of Acquiring That Which One Desires 155

Simply Put, What Does It Mean To Heal Through Energy?

Energy healing, also known as Reiki in some parts of the world, is a form of complementary and alternative medicine in which practitioners of the practice use their hands to transfer the energy of the cosmos from themselves to their patients.

If you're curious about how it works, the practitioner of energy healing is meant to use their hands as an instrument of therapy in order to tap into the energy fields that surround the body. The Japanese terms rei (universal) and ki (mystery environment) are the origin of the term reiki, which translates to "life energy." The goal of energy healing is to infuse one's body and spirit with the same energy that permeates the cosmos.

According to many who practice energy healing, places in the body where there has been either physical or emotional suffering might make it easy for energy to become trapped there. This energy almost always has a negative effect on both our bodily and mental health; hence, we would want to rid ourselves of it and bring the body's equilibrium back to normal.

SECTION B B) HOW TO CREATE OPEN HEAVENS How to create open heavens

a) A DECREE CONdemning Powers Active in the First and Second Heavens

"For we do not wrestle against flesh and blood, but rather against principalities, against powers, against the rulers of the darkness of this world, and against spiritual wickedness in high places," the Bible says.12th verse of Ephesians

A few of the powers that function in the universe are housed in the second heaven, which is symbolic of the atmosphere and the air. Satan, also known as the prince of the air, and those working for him make use of the powers that are described here. Therefore, the purpose of these abilities is to create barriers that prevent the prayers of many believers from reaching God, who resides in the third heaven. They achieve this goal by producing some wicked projections that will result in a great deal of distraction, so preventing the target from benefiting from the blessings that heaven has to offer. Some of these things include causing someone to oversleep to the point that they miss prayer, as well as different kinds of crimes that have to do with the body, such as fornication or adultery, which can lead to one being bound in servitude.

It would therefore be beneficial if you decreed against such powers that they will not obstruct your path to the seat of grace. You are to speak words of authority against them in the name of Jesus, and you are to command that their actions be turned into foolishness for the sake of you.

It is written in 1 Corinthians 14:2 that when I speak in tongues, I cause confusion among them. Because of this, I speak in tongues more often.

Because no one will be able to understand you if you speak in tongues, you will be communicating only with God if you have this ability. You will state that it was done via the power of the Spirit, yet everything will remain a mystery.

The mysterious one communicates with you when you speak in tongues, which causes the agent of darkness to become confused and causes them to run when you do so. When they hear one utter that, they don't grasp what you're saying to your Father because the prayer is from one's Spirit to his creator, God almighty. Therefore, they run away from you because they don't understand what you're saying.

This is one method for clearing them out and causing the sky above you to open up.

PRAYER DESTINATIONS

a) Pray for an open heaven; b) Pray for deliverance from the works of darkness; and c) Pray that the adversary's plot to lead you astray into temptation will never be successful.

d) Pray for the discernment spirit to be able to dictate the appearance of evil around you. e) Pray that your inner man, which is also called the spirit man, receives fire. f) Cover yourself with the blood of Jesus as you pray. g) Pray to receive divine strength. h) Pray for easy access to his throne of grace without hindrance. i) Pray that you may be able to see clearly. j) Pray that you may

c) THE DESTROYING OF EVIL YOKES

"Is not this the fast that I choose, to loosen the bonds of wickedness, to undo the bands of the yoke, and to let the oppressed go free...and to break every yoke...?..."Isaiah 58:6 [Verse]

Declare that every harmful yoke that has been placed against your ability to receive from above is broken in the name of Jesus. The yoke may take the form of lack of resources, shame, illness, or a delay in achieving achievements. They were conceived by your oppressors, who do not wish for you to advance in any way, shape, or form. It is necessary to pray against it in order to have open heavens.

If the Holy Spirit prompts you to, you can perform this prayer while anointing yourself with oil. When used in the appropriate manner, anointing oil can be effective in freeing people from oppressive yokes.

One woman had a hard time finding someone to spend the rest of her life with, so she went to a lot of different religious events, where there were even men who claimed to be praying for her, but nothing worked. After a long period of time comprised of months and years, she grew weary of participating in religious activities. After that, she made the decision to spend some alone time with the Lord. When she had finished praying, she poured some of the anointing oil into the air and summoned her destined companion for life. During that month, she started dating a man, and a few years later, they tied the knot, and they continue to enjoy wedded bliss to this day. The yoke was broken when that anointing oil was released into the air, and as a result, she had an unusual result, which is a heavenly connection with the person who will one day be her spouse. The presence of a malevolent yoke was the obstacle that prevented her from getting together with him. When this kind of thing was presented to me in the realm of Spirit, it appeared to be a black coverage in the realm of Spirit that can force two people to not meet with each other even though they are close to each other. This form of projection is carried out by the devil and his agent, most commonly when they wish to create obstacles or delay in the life of someone who is looking for a future mate or who is hoping to meet someone who can help them fulfill their destiny.

The anointing destroys it, and something that initially appears to be very challenging will, in the end, turn out to be very straightforward.

PRAYER POINTS a) Pray that evil yokes against blessings are broken b) Pray against any form of delay or setback in your life and family c) Pray for divine connection d) Pray also for divine promotion e) Pray for a divine appointment with your destiny helper f) Pray for the speedy manifestation of your blessings g) Pray for overflows and abundance in your life h) Pray for opened doors PRAYER POINT

Filmmaking In The Mind

Have you tried to bring more optimism into your life, only to find that the outcomes left you feeling disappointed, frustrated, or uninspired? If so, this could be why. If you answered yes to any of these questions, you are NOT alone! It is a really tragic and depressing reality that the vast majority of people will never get the kind of transcendent and life-changing experiences they seek as a result of participating in activities related to the Law of Attraction. This is the stark truth.

The plain and straightforward fact is that visualization is effective! It works effectively, it works rapidly, and it works for absolutely everyone.

You should not give up on anything simply because you haven't had success with it in the past.

Mind movies are a fairly new phenomenon that have swept the online in recent months, but in reality, they are just a terrific way of utilizing modern technology to ageless knowledge and truths. In recent months, mind movies have swept the internet.

The Photographs

They have a very straightforward method of operation. Your mind movies serve as a visual picture of the ideal life that you have envisioned for yourself. Your best possible self. Your best self, and in the settings that are most significant...the life that you'd most like to be leading at this very moment.

Visual aids for personal growth and development, or "mind movies" as they are more commonly known in the fields of spiritual healing and other therapies. They consist of personally selected (or mass manufactured) positive visual pictures of a person's ideal existence, as well as written or vocal positive affirmation about a person and their life.

Positive thoughts that are formed by viewing or listening to mind movies will work as a large eraser, which we may use to erase, then substitute damaging programming that is stored in our brains. These thoughts can be generated by either watching or listening to mind movies.

Making your own "mind movie" can be accomplished in a variety of different ways. From creating the image of your ideal life in a large scrap book or on a cork board, to developing complex internet software that is self-driven.

When it comes to anything in life, the amount of work you put in is what matters the most, and the more creativity you put into it, the greater the effect it will have on both your conscious and subconscious minds.

There are many circumstances that, in the course of an average person's life, will either provide or produce detrimental energetic effects, such as dampening the spirit, stockpiling negativity, and ultimately turning into negative or disempowering beliefs, which, in turn, will produce detrimental emotional reactions, which, if they are persisted in and endured for a sufficient amount of time, may cause psychosomatic illness.

To put it another way, unpleasant emotional states that are maintained for extended periods of time will eventually solidify in the body in the form of a disease, either physical or mental, which will prevent us from having the life that we want.

Whether it be the person who is seemingly always there to let you know that you can't achieve or the obstacles that appear to be unattainable regardless of how hard we strive, the use of mind movies may be a powerful tool that may be used in the process of breaking the destructive pattern that has developed in one's life.

You can make your own film with the help of online tools, or you can make your own vision book, which is a collection of images depicting your objective, an ideal position you want to find yourself in, business accomplishments, romantic goals, or anything else you can think of.

Using these, you will work toward the goal of combining and rearranging positive affirmations, which are condensed expressions of desires that you hope may one day be realized. If you are utilizing a software solution that is accessible online, you will have the ability to select your own song.

Engage with what you see and hear on each level as you watch the film you've produced, read through your vision book, or stand in front of your vision board.

The foundation of this principle is the idea that you should focus on what it is that you want to the exclusion of all else, which is the most potent force in the universe. The age-old proverb that "energy flows where attention goes" is, without a doubt, accurate.

Maintain A Relationship With The Person Of Christ

John 15: 1 "My Father is the gardener, and I am the proper vine," the proverb goes. 2 It's possible that some of the branches that make up me don't have any fruit on them. Consequently, my father will trim those branches. In addition to this, he prunes back every branch that bears fruit. He trims each and every one of those branches so that they would produce more fruit. 3 You have already been made clean as a result of the words that I have spoken to you.

4 Keep living in me, and I'll keep living in you as long as you keep living in me. By itself, a branch is unable to produce fruit. Only if it remains attached to the vine will it have the ability to produce fruit. You are the same in that regard. You can't bear fruit until you stay rooted in me for the foreseeable future.' 5 "I am the vine, and you are the branches," the Lord said to them. You have to stay a part of me, and I have to

be a part of you. You will only be successful in producing a large quantity of fruit if you do that. This is due to the fact that without me you are unable to accomplish anything. 6 If anybody does not continue to be a part of me, then that person is analogous to a withered branch. That branch is going to be thrown away by the gardener, and eventually it will become dry. People will take those withered branches and toss them into the fire. Therefore, the dry branches catch fire. (Easy English). Beloved, a songwriter once stated that if you choose to live your life apart from Christ, you will find yourself stuck in shifting sand. Simply said, it indicates that we are unable to triumph over the devil with only our own resources. It suggests that we ought to depend entirely on God for the supply of His skills, which will make it possible for us to receive good things and blessings from God, and we ought to do this in a continuous manner.

Listen as the Lord Jesus Christ makes the audacious declaration that He, Jesus Christ, is the true vine, and that His Father is the gardener. According to what the Bible has to say, Jesus Christ is the true vine, and we are the branches that grow off of it. This is a wonderful term that needs to be correctly segmented in order to facilitate simple assimilation. Because the Lord Jesus Christ is the true vine and we are his branches, it follows that we now share in the divine nature that He possesses.

This indicates that the life, power, anointing, and righteousness of the Lord Jesus Christ are currently being transmitted to us in a direct manner. According to research in agriculture, a vine and a branch both belong to the same tree and are mutually dependent on each other for their continued existence. Through its roots, the vine is able to obtain minerals and water from the surrounding soil, which helps the tree to maintain its youthful appearance. The energy from the sun is absorbed by the branches of the vine, where it is then converted into chlorophyll and used in the process of photosynthesis, which makes it possible for the plant to continue growing.

This is the character of the connection that we have with God through our Lord Jesus Christ, and it is a wonderful thing. The eternal life that we have was given to us by Christ, but the heavenly Father is the one who gives us life. The instant we acknowledge Jesus as our Lord and Savior, we are grafted into the supernatural life that God has created for those who believe in him. At that particular moment, God intends to utilize us as his branches to produce fruit, and he is looking for ways to do so. The fulfillment of God's aspirations for us is to produce fruit that will lead to the salvation of more people and the expansion of his kingdom. It is necessary for the Kingdom of God to grow, and we are the vehicles through which God will accomplish this task. It is important that we do not let God down. We need to strengthen our commitment to the Lord in order to increase the amount of fruit we produce and thereby contribute to the expansion of God's kingdom.

Believers are being admonished by the Lord Jesus Christ to continue to live in Him (Jesus Christ), and when we do so, He will also continue to live in us. This is because when we remain in Him, He will continue to live in us. Dearly Beloved, are you able to fathom the magnitude of the blessing that the awakening of this consciousness bestows upon us? If you continue to stay in the Lord, he will eventually make his dwelling place in you, and then, well, you can probably guess what happens next: you will enter a realm where you have access to all kinds of supernatural skills. During his mission on earth, the Lord Jesus was accompanied by a supernatural presence, and he is communicating to us now that if we want to experience the same magnitude of supernatural talents that he did, then we must continue to abide in him. Please don't cut yourself off from Him, and you can be sure of one thing: the power of God will manifest in your life in a way that is stress-free if you don't disconnect from him.

Because the branch cannot produce fruit on its own, it is necessary for us to remain in Him as our source of life. Only if the branch stays attached to the vine will it be able to produce fruit in the future. It is important to keep in mind that the Scriptures are discussing our relationship with Christ. It suggests that we are in this manner. If we do not continue to dwell or abide in Christ, who is the actual vine, then we will not produce fruit. After he had finished his lengthy discourse, the Lord Jesus emphasized to his followers and to everyone who would later come to believe on His name that He is the true vine, and that we are the branches that bear fruit from that vine. We need to continue to dwell in Jesus Christ so that he can continue to dwell in us. Because of this, we will have the ability to meet the difficulties posed by the adversary and emerge victorious.

Ephesians 1:22 should be read. Everything is subject to Christ's authority since God has put everything beneath his feet. Christ has been elevated by God to the position of chief executive officer and head of his people, the church. (Simplified English)

Don't be afraid; the answer is quite close to you. Do you want to be able to exercise authority over the powers of darkness? Maintain a connection to the teachings of the Master Jesus Christ and his person. The power that belongs to the heavenly Father has been completely transferred to the Lord Jesus Christ. It follows that if you are not connected to Jesus Christ, you will not have access to the strength that God has provided for you. In the event that your fellowship is severed, the Bible instructs us to keep our connection to Jesus strong.

Jesus Christ, the Lord, is in charge of the administration of all of heaven's riches, as God has appointed him to do so. In point of fact, what this phrase is implying is that Christ now has control over everything. He is the only person on whom God may legitimately bestow His authority. Christ is the head of everything pertaining to God's people, the church, and he has been appointed by God as the leader of the new creation. Therefore, we are obligated to follow our leader, Christ, and submit ourselves to the directives he gives us. If we do this, we will be able to carry out the assignments on His mandate that will make us happy and joyful. Staying connected to the Lord and trusting in his will for your life will ensure that you experience joy while serving God, which in turn will make the manifestation of the supernatural easier for you.

Take a look at Colossians 1:18. Imagine the people who follow Christ as Christ's body. Christ sits at the helm of that particular assembly. It is commonly referred to as the church. He is where everything starts. And the Son that the Father has given to the world is him. Therefore, he is the leader of everyone who is going to triumph over death in the battle. As a direct consequence of this, Christ occupies the position of utmost priority in everything. (Simplified English)

Beloved, we are a unique people; in fact, the Bible refers to us as God's new creation. As members of God's chosen people, we have been fashioned in Christ Jesus. Because Christ is the Son of the Father, anybody who professes faith in Jesus automatically meets the requirements to become a son of God and is eligible to receive his portion of the inheritance that is reserved for the saints of God. Therefore, he is the leader of everyone who confesses faith in Christ, and the most effective approach to triumph over death is to maintain a connection with Him and to faithfully execute His instructions. Your victory over all of Satan's armies will be certain if you obey the Lord and do what he says.

Ephesians 1:10 should be read. When the time is absolutely perfect, God will accomplish what he set out to do. Then, all things, both those in heaven and those on earth, will be brought together under his control. God will eventually unite everything under the authority of Jesus Christ, who will serve as the head of the church. 15 People have told me about the way in which you maintain your faith in Jesus Christ as Lord. They have conveyed to me that you have affection for each and every one of God's people. As a result of the fact that I have been told these things about you, (Simplified English)

Ephesians 5:23 should be read. Because a husband is the head of his wife, just as Christ is the head of the church, which is another name for the people who follow him (his people). Christ's body, which is the church, is the recipient of his atoning work. (Simplified English)

Every One Of Us Is Interconnected

Today, you are guaranteed to run into at least one familiar face no matter where you travel. Additionally, that individual will know a number of people who know an even greater number of people, and eventually the circle of individuals will return to someone who already knows you. The cliche that "the world is a small place" is, in fact, accurate. But what if our connections ran far deeper than that? Along with fluids, bones, tissues, and muscles, the human body is also composed of energy in the form of light, vibrations, and frequencies. Our bodies are made up of this energy. The fact that we can occasionally give someone a shock after walking across carpeting is evidence that every person has a certain amount of electrical current that travels through them. As a result of this, we are aware that every person has a certain amount of electrical current that passes through them. As a result, because we are all made of electricity, we are a component of a larger whole in the cosmos, which means that we are all related to one another. Because we have never been shown how to engage with that aspect of ourselves, we are simply unaware of the link that exists between us.

Because this is how we have been taught to engage with other people, the majority of our lives are spent just communicating with other people on a surface level. The majority of us are under the impression that we were conceived of and brought into existence at some point in time far in the past by a being or power that is superior to ourselves. Because this is how we have been instructed to communicate with higher power, we may periodically pray or meditate in an effort to make contact with it. Only the information that our professors already know can be passed on to us. At some point in our lives, we start to look for new information and become exposed to new points of view.

During this process, we occasionally come to the realization that the things we have always known are not always all there is to know about a subject. You are about to go on a journey that will bring you to new levels of enlightenment, and this is that adventure.

Because of the force that was responsible for our creation, we are inextricably linked with one another. That power, no matter what name you choose to call it, did not create us and then turn its back on us and walk away, leaving us to struggle in a world full of turmoil and sorrow. This is true regardless of the name you choose to give it. This force is both within of us and all around us; it is a part of our conscious and unconscious thought, and it is limitless in its capacity to transform your life into the life you have always fantasized about living. Once you have been instructed on how to tap into the powers that surround you each and every second of every single day, all you have to do is think about your requirements and wishes, and everything will fall into place. Because there is a correct method to use this power as well as an incorrect way to use it, it is a skill that needs to be taught and something that needs to be used with judgment. You will see how the connections effect not only your life, but how it can and should be used to better the lives of everyone that you come into contact with as well, once you have mastered the skills and have the power to make changes happen in your life. This will become apparent once you have the ability to make changes happen in your life.

We are connected to this power, and therefore we are connected to everything that this power has ever produced as a result of that connection. Just take a little stroll outside and take stock of your immediate environment. In the natural world, there is a certain spot and role for everything. In nature, nothing is ever wasted because, once it has fulfilled its purpose, it is recycled by the laws of nature and either becomes something else or supports the existence of another creature. This ensures that nothing in nature is ever thrown away. You, too, are a part of this cycle, and you hold a position within the natural order of things. Every choice you make in life will, in some way, influence the people and events that occur in the world around you. Some of your acts will seem insignificant to you, and neither you nor anyone else will notice them in any way. However, it is possible that nature itself will take notice of certain deeds, while others will make an impression on other people. The power that fashioned us is keeping track of all of your activities. If you were to stop and think about the repercussions of these activities on a molecular level, it would be so taxing on the mind that it would cause you to become completely inactive. As a result, as a species, we do not stop to think about how our actions affect the environment around us on such a profound level of interaction. It is precisely this ability to think about our actions that presents the greatest challenge for us when we are attempting to feel connected to other people and to the world around us. The things that take place in our everyday lives that appear to be miraculous can frequently be explained away as the result of chance, karma, or even just plain old good luck. We have been socialized to believe that miracles do not occur to the average person, and as a result, we are incapable of recognizing a miracle when it takes place in our own lives. By failing to recognize a miracle for what it truly is and by failing to understand that it is our connection with everything else in the universe that enables these miracles to occur for us, we reduce the likelihood that we will be blessed with more frequent occurrences of miracles.

Because of our link to this greater force, everything that takes place in our lives, the world around us, and the environment in which we find ourselves is ultimately caused by this connection.

This higher force protects the humble toad and the delicate butterfly from the dangers of the world so that they don't have to worry about living their lives. The animals that live in the wild do not have to worry about issues related to friendships or even their own sustenance. Because we think about everything to the point of exhaustion, and because we have not yet learned that we can ask this greater force for the same kind of gifts for our own existence, we humans, unfortunately, are constantly preoccupied with anxieties and concerns. It goes without saying that we work hard to ensure that we have sufficient housing and food, but we don't stop there. We always want more than we need to exist, and at times we even have the mistaken belief that we deserve more than we have because we work so hard. Stop thinking that we are the reason we have anything at all and we will be one step closer to true oneness with our higher power, the universe, or whatever it is that we believe in that is bigger than ourselves. This is necessary if we are to achieve true oneness with these things. Because of the grace of this higher force, we were able to obtain everything that we do have today. This is the reason why we are so successful.

When people lose everything they own as a result of natural calamities, an immediate need for assistance is made. When people from different parts of the world reach out to one another in order to offer support and to help another person, a small but significant step toward global oneness is taken. The vast majority of individuals would not consider this a second chance or an opportunity to begin over. It's possible that this is the method the cosmos is trying to reset people's futures for them. Many people who find themselves in these kinds of predicaments find that they end up with something better than they had to begin with, or that they end up getting the opportunity to make some major change in their life that they had been using excuses to put off until this major disaster came along and took everything that was holding them back and swept it all away. In either case, they were able to find some silver lining in what seemed to be an otherwise dark cloud. There are moments when life smacks us above the head and tells us, "Hey, look, you're going about this all the wrong way, so let's just start over." At this point, you should be able to observe the beginning of your oneness with the other people, but instead, you fail to recognize your oneness with the cosmos and the higher power. Why? mostly due to the fact that we have been socialized to believe what can only be seen with one's own eyes. Some people believe that if something can't be observed, then it must not be real; nevertheless, this is not the case. When you are able to relax to the point where you are ready to believe that you can be one with the entire universe and have a daily oneness with your higher power, you will find that the things you cannot see will deliver the greatest life-changing miracles of all. When you are able to do this, you will realize that you can be one with the entire universe. The actual magic will start to happen at that moment, and your hopes and wishes will start to become a reality.

Have Faith In The Law Of Attraction's (Loa) Power, And Don't Be Afraid To Dream Big.

You must have faith in the power of the Law of Attraction (LOA) as well as the power of your own mind, and you must never stop dreaming big in order to accomplish significant things in your life. If you are not absolutely certain that you will receive what you want and that you are deserving of what you want, you will always have a difficult time accomplishing what it is that you desire.

The fact that Stephen King's manuscripts were rejected on multiple occasions and thrown out by publishers almost led him to believe that he wasn't destined to be a writer. However, he persisted and eventually became successful. He made the conscious decision to have faith in himself, in the power of the universe, and in the principle that you can bring into existence everything you believe in. He refused to let the humiliation of being turned down stop him from pursuing his dreams, and as a result, his first novel was eventually published. After that initial breakthrough, he went on to have a string of subsequent victories, and before long, there was no turning back for him.

There are an infinite number of examples of this, and each one of them plainly demonstrates the strength that comes from thinking big and believing that your dreams can come true.

How to Have Big Dreams while Still Believing in Your Own Dreams?

If you want something badly enough, you can get it, regardless of how outlandish or impossible the goal may appear. To put the law of attraction to work for you in a positive manner, it is essential to allow your thoughts to meander in as many different areas as possible, generate a variety of ideas, and eventually zero in on something that you genuinely desire. If you give yourself permission to dream big without placing any restrictions on the scope of those dreams, you will be in a better position to identify the aspiration in which you have unwavering faith and which you would most like to see realized in your life.

When you think you want something, give yourself permission to dream as big as you possibly can, even if achieving some of your goals seems absolutely unachievable to you. You have to rid your mind of the word "impossible" since your preoccupation with it has kept you from reaching your full potential all these years. You felt how certain things were not possible, and you believed that certain goals had restrictions; as a result, you continued reducing them and making them more realistic so that you might at least reach them.

The difficulty with this strategy is that when you modify your ambitions too much, you remove the element of 'excitement' from them. This is because the 'large,' 'risky,' 'almost impossible,' and 'too difficult' aspects of the objective were what made it unique to you in the first place. Believe it or not, but that is exactly why you felt enthused about that objective, and if you removed all of those parts from it, it wouldn't be the same to you. If you remove all of those elements, it wouldn't be the same to you.

How can you be enthusiastic about just singing opera at a small theater in a town that nobody knows about if you've always wanted to be the best opera singer in your country and play at the top opera houses and theaters in the world? Naturally, taking advantage of that opportunity would make you feel good as well; however, if that is not what you want to do, you will become exhausted very quickly.

You have to give yourself permission to think big thoughts and dream big dreams because only then will you be able to recognize your genuine requirements and have faith in them. If you want to dream large, write down everything you want and continue to describe it in detail as you go. Do not give up at any time, even if you believe that a particular concept is unachievable. Keep writing about your most profound and significant yearnings, and whenever you do so, make sure to do so with a grin on your face since this demonstrates that you have faith in the process.

Set Goals

A true winner is someone who is self-aware enough to know what they want out of life and is prepared to sacrifice whatever it takes to achieve their goals. They have a clear vision of what they want out of life, and they are willing to sacrifice anything in order to get it. The question now is, how exactly do you go about doing that? You need to give some thought to the goals that you have set for yourself in this life. Think about the means by which you will obtain not only what you actually desire but also what it is that you want. It's possible that figuring things out will take a little bit more time than you initially anticipated, but don't worry; the payoff will be well worth it. You'll be able to achieve the goals that you've always dreamed of and some that you may never have even believed possible.

Take a look at your life and consider where you would like to be at this same time the following month. What about this same time the following year? What about the future in five years' time? Or even ten? Or perhaps even 20 in total? Take out a piece of paper and write down what you would like to accomplish in life that would make you able to look back on your life and be perfectly happy. Those things are the goals that you have for your future and the rest of your life. You will be better prepared to achieve them if you write them down and keep them in mind. If you're a little skeptical that's fine, but it's actually entirely true. You may be surprised about it but just by writing down those goals your mind thinks about the more clearly and is more likely to believe in them. This makes it more likely also that you will actually accomplish th

The fact of the matter is that all of us are somewhat visually-oriented people. We think, "Oh, it would be nice to have a new car," but unless we start truly reaching for and deciding, "I will have a new car," we really don't end up with what we want in the way that we want it. We don't end up with what we want in the way that we want it. It's possible that we'll never get that new car because we never even tried to acquire it. Now is the moment to stop wishing for things and start working toward something instead.

Winners are the ones who set goals. They choose the goals that they desire to achieve in their lifetime. In addition to this, they devise strategies for accomplishing those objectives. Therefore, set out a few minutes to go over your list and check off everything you want to accomplish. Are you going to be able to check everything off your list? In all honesty, there is no way to find out. On the other hand, if you take the initiative and begin working for them, there is every chance that you will be able to. You have taken the first step forward by putting them down on paper.

Taking the second step, which is actually establishing a strategy for how you are going to attain them, is the second step, and it is the way that you are going to improve yourself even more.

Get directly to work on such plans as soon as possible. The sooner you come up with them and put them into practice, the better it will be for you in the long run. You will be able to actually achieve the objectives that you have set for yourself, and then you will be able to move on to establishing new objectives. Additionally, each time you really accomplish a goal that you have set for yourself, it is going to make you feel even better about yourself and even better about your capacity to reach other goals in the future. This is because you will be able to see that not only is it feasible in general, but it is also possible for you specifically. This will make you feel more confident in your ability to reach other goals in the future.

After all is said and done, our goals are what shape us into the individuals we aspire to be. Consider the implications. How exactly did you go about getting the job that you had your heart set on? How were you able to acquire the grades that you want when you were in school? You gave yourself goals to pursue, and after you decided what those goals were, you worked as hard as you possibly could to make them a reality. When you don't give yourself goals to work toward, it's already a challenge to get anything done. But it gets considerably more difficult. What is the cause? You do not possess any of them. You see, when you don't have the motivation to do something or when you aren't striving for anything, you just don't get as much done. Winners are continually working toward achieving something, whether that goal is significant or unimportant.

Medicreation

I like to refer to this as "deliberate deja vu" because you are "rehearsing" your vision in your mind as you imagine it. One of the most challenging aspects of bringing into existence what you desire is convincing yourself that you already own it. In light of this, it is essential to locate the "sweet spot" each time you engage in exercise. The optimal zone is the region in which you have the sensation that you are ACTUALLY experiencing whatever it is that you are striving to bring into existence. There are others who believe that this is the moment when the third eye is fully opened. It is a state in which one's imagination is so intensely vivid and vividly intense that it seems more real than everything that one sees when opening their eyes. It may take you twenty minutes to an hour to locate this, but with experience, you can find it nearly instantaneously (sometimes), and as a result, you should play with it multiple times a day if you are able to do so.

You can't Medicreate if your body and brain are not relaxed, therefore you can't do it while you're washing the dishes (but you can see your vision and cause yourself to experience happy while you're washing the dishes!). It is necessary for us to disconnect ourselves from our outward worlds in order to be able to create openly and intently within our interior worlds. This is your opportunity to create a picture of what you want, and then to make that picture a reality. You won't be able to accomplish that task when the dog is licking your foot and the children are watching too loud of a Sponge Bob episode on television. It is absolutely necessary to acquire headphones or designate a certain location in which you can be alone. If you are unable to bring the images in your mind to life to the point where you can feel them in your body, then all you are doing is daydreaming, and that didn't get Walter

Mitty very far, did it? "My brain is only a receiver; in the universe, there is a core from which we obtain information, strength, and inspiration." Although I have not explored the innermost recesses of this center, I am aware that it is there. Tesla, Nikola

Medicreation, in its most basic form, is a combination of imagination, meditation, and conscious creation. It provides all of the benefits that traditional meditation does, but it also includes a massive shortcut and a super cool quantum physics component. This not only enables you to override negative neural programming, but it also assists you in consciously and subconsciously creating what you want in your life. That must have been a tough pill to swallow.

When we disconnect from the outside world, slow down our brain waves, relax our bodies, create an image that represents our Ideal Outcome, and bring up the emotion of already having that outcome realized, we are changing the neurological structure of our brains, the biochemical structure of our bodies, and the very reality that we are a part of on a quantum conscious level.

It seems straightforward, doesn't it? Because our naturally critical brains have a tendency to prevent us from embracing this idea, it is helpful to keep in mind that it is founded not only on science but also on sacred writings.

During the Medicreation process, what you are doing in reality is taking your Ideal Outcome and supplementing it with some happy feelings. You will utilize your imagination in such a way that you will be able to persuade your subconscious mind (and, by extension, your body and your brain) that you have already accomplished the Ideal Outcome that you are seeing once you have reached a state of mental and physical relaxation. In the field of quantum research, where space and time do not exist, it is important to remember that your Medicreation is more of a discovery than it is a creation. The same branch of science tells us that if we witness something, we have an effect on it; therefore, it is your responsibility to notice your enhanced reality in your mind so that it can manifest itself as tangible stuff (which isn't really tangible anyhow).

Naturally, we will also make advantage of the potent good emotions we are currently experiencing in order to biochemically inundate our bodies with feelings of thankfulness. All of this will start to override any negative ideas you have while also providing you with the fuel and bravery to take significant actions toward achieving your goals. To put it another way, that is Medicreation in a nutshell.

Before I break this down for you into simple steps, I want you to keep in mind that simply reading about something is not the same as actually engaging in that activity. I simply cannot emphasize this point enough. You might believe that you do not have the time to set aside a few minutes each morning or evening (the optimal times) to carry out your own version of Medicreation, but this is always a decision that you have. Really, how much time do we waste fussing with our hair or watching old episodes of our favorite shows? And don't even get me started on wasting my time with ad breaks! You can put in as much effort as you want, but this one thing will help you create your vision more than anything else. I apologize, since I am aware that you may enjoy watching Games of Thrones, but that is a work of fiction, and this is your life, which you have the ability to make SO MUCH BETTER if you so want. When something is done in the right way and with consistency, the benefits will become apparent. Always keep in mind that you are the one who is constructing your life, regardless of whether or not you are conscious of this fact; therefore, you may as well think about your life the way you want it to be, wouldn't you agree?

This information can be more easily retained if you refer to it by its acronym, D.I.C.E. The fundamental breakdown is presented first, followed by a more in-depth discussion of each individual phase. Once you have an understanding of how straightforward this is, you will be able to use it to rewrite any old programming that may be preventing you from achieving your objectives, as well as to establish new neural networks that will (re)wire you to work toward achieving those objectives. As a side note, the inspiration for this acronym comes from a comment attributed to Albert Einstein: "God doesn't play dice with the Universe."

How To Get More Energy To Meet Your Needs

There are a number of different approaches you may take to boost your vibratory levels and make the Law of Attraction function more effectively for you. Here are just a few of them, but by the time you have experimented with all of these and incorporated them into your everyday life, you will also find other strategies that will come to you as a natural progression as a consequence of your constant learning and developing. These techniques will come to you as a result of your constant learning and growing. Here are just a few of them.

Raise the frequency of your belief in your own capacity for success by raising your vibrational level.

People who have confidence in themselves and their abilities have an easier time convincing others. These are the kinds of people who go on to become successful business owners, but they didn't get there by chance. They were able to get there because they believed in themselves and their potential to achieve their goals and realize their ambitions. Bill Gates is a well-known example of a person who followed his dreams and believed in himself. He had a strong conviction that people might be brought together via the use of computers, and he was able to make this vision a reality through the creation of Microsoft. On the other hand, he did not immediately succeed in persuading others. He encountered some resistance. In point of fact, the bank that he approached for financial assistance in the early stages of his company's existence denied his request for assistance. He never stopped believing that his dream would come true, and now that it has, he is working harder than ever to make it an even more ambitious goal. Why? Because he was confident in his abilities to make his aspirations and goals come true and he was aware that they could be made into reality.

Your degree of self-belief can be increased if you have clear aspirations and objectives concerning the things you want out of life, and if you then make a concerted effort each day to move in the direction of achieving those aspirations and objectives. Every time a person has a sense of achievement or completion, regardless of the size of the accomplishment or whether or not it is related to the person's goals, their level of self-esteem rises. Simply getting into the routine of making your bed right after you wake up each morning is all it takes to boost your feelings of accomplishment, which in turn enhances your levels of self-esteem and self-confidence, which in turn raises the frequency of your vibrations. Because it demonstrates to your mind and the universe that you have the ability to complete and follow through with things, you will eventually start to believe that you can make anything you could possibly desire come to fruition if you demonstrate that you are capable of doing so by completing small tasks such as this one. This is essential to your success in reaching your larger goals and dreams. If you are unable to exercise self-control in order to complete even the most menial of activities, it is quite probable that you will have difficulty achieving the more significant goals that you have set for yourself in life.

You won't be able to get what you want if you step on other people to acquire it, but you may show gratitude to the individuals who help you along the way and trust that the positive interactions you seek will be provided to you as a gift from the universe. You will face difficulties on your path to manifestation, but know that these difficulties are the Universe's way of determining whether or not you truly deserve what it is that you desire – they are a test to determine whether or not you are willing to make sacrifices and persevere through difficult times because you believe that the end result will be well worth it.

A considerable increase in one's vibrational frequencies can be attained by the everyday practice of expressing gratitude to or for anybody or anything. This can also be accomplished through one's belief in oneself. Those that go through life with a constructive mentality and an optimistic perspective already experience it at a higher vibratory level than those who do not.

The Key to Your Success Is Meditation

You can attain whatever it is that you want to achieve by developing a greater level of mental control via the practice of meditation on a regular basis. This mental control can be developed through the usage of your ideas. What exactly is meditation, then? For the time being, all you need to know is that it is basically training your mind to be able to see things for what they are and without judgment and to develop more of an ease to hone in on inner connection between the body and the mind. The elaboration of meditation, including all of its proven health benefits, is sufficient to cover the contents of another book. This is of tremendous assistance in increasing the overall vibrational frequency of your body! Not to mention the fact that meditation lowers stress levels in both the mind and the body, which helps to diminish some of the potentially bad vibrations that you are putting out into the world and replaces them with much more upbeat and optimistic feelings.

Kindness Acts and Deeds

Kindness that comes with the expectation of receiving anything in return is not genuine kindness since it comes with a cost, and when you exhibit this behavior, you give off the low frequencies associated with greed and selfishness. Your vibrational frequencies will increase and you will be able to tap into the abundant resources of the universe when you raise the frequency of your kindness and generosity out of love for others, without any expectation of receiving anything in return. You will also be able to have a far more positive outlook on who you are as a result of doing this. Set yourself the challenge of being good to at least three different individuals every day without anticipating any form of acknowledgement or gratitude in return. Do not brag about the nice things you have done; rather, contribute with a spirit of generosity. When you are able to achieve that, you will be able to dominate the world because the height of your vibrational levels will be such that you will be able to attract anything into your life that you have ever desired!

While you are making more of an effort to give, it is important that you remember to leave room in your heart to receive as well. If you close yourself up to the possibility of obtaining wonderful things in life, how can you possibly believe that it will bring you anything worthwhile? There is always a donor and there is always a receiver in the cycle of energy flow; this is how it works. There is no such thing as giving if one does not first receive. The concept of "taking" from others, whether in the form of accepting presents, favors, compliments, or anything else, can make a lot of people uncomfortable. However, if one maintains such a mentality, it is impossible to be more incorrect. If you consistently close yourself off to the love and positive energy that people have to offer, it is unreasonable to anticipate that your life will produce positive outcomes for you. That will only make it more difficult for you to realize your ambitions through the use of the Law of Attraction.

Things Which Get In The Way Of Your Manifestation

your desires is a necessary component for the realisation of your aspirations. It is impossible to bring about the things you seek if you do not have trust.

If you could have anything in life that your heart desired, what kind of mentality would you have? What kinds of thoughts, feelings, and conversations would you have about yourself? Would you change the way that you walk and dress? Would you still consider yourself to be broke even if you had a million dollars in the bank? Would you continue to engage in the same behaviors you did when you had no money, or would you behave differently now that you have a lot of it?

The following are three factors that stand in the way of your manifestation:

Lack of belief.

Now is the time to triumph over any and all unbelief that stands in the way of the materialization of your dreams. Because of your lack of faith, no matter how hard you try to make the things you want come true, you won't be able to do it no matter how much effort you put into it.

Unbelief is the primary cause of the paralysis that affects our hearts. The most faithful among us will be saved by faith, while the most unbelieving among us will be destroyed by unbelief. If you talk about not believing, you will end up believing; if you talk about believing, you will end up believing. It's not always easy to have faith, but if you keep taking those baby steps of trust, you'll slowly start to see that your faith is developing.

Careless conversation.

The power of words much exceeds anything you could ever hope to fathom. Whatever it is that you say aloud, that is exactly what you will bring to you. People will sometimes speak without thinking before they do so. The fact that you talked carelessly but didn't truly mean what you said did not in any way undermine the effectiveness of the said words, nor would it liberate you from being held accountable for them. Rather, the fact that you talked carelessly but didn't genuinely mean what you said did not negate the effectiveness of the spoken words.

Your words hold the ability to determine the course of your life. When spoken, words grab hold of listeners and begin to develop into their full potential. They have the potential to bring out either beneficial or harmful fruits. The use of positive language will result in the production of positive fruits. On the other hand, negative words bring about negative outcomes. Whatever it is that you put your words into action to create, you will get back.

You must have faith that your goals will become a reality before you can even begin to pursue them. You have the ability to bring about positive changes in any facet of your life that you choose. Your words have the power to bring about real change, so watch how you use them and avoid being reckless.

Fear.

We were not given the spirit of fear by God, but rather the spirit of power, love, and a clear mind. The only place that fear can be found is in a person's head. Your anxieties are the source of the roadblocks in the way of your manifestation. On the other side of fear lies everything you could possibly want. If you continue to let fear rule your life, you will never be able to have faith that is unshakeable and you will never be able to speak up for the causes that are important to you. Because you allow fear to control your life, you will never be able to live the life of your dreams.

The worries that you don't confront end up defining your capabilities. You won't be able to start living the life of your dreams until you finally conquer your fears and put them behind you for good. Confronting your anxieties is the only way to ensure that nothing can stop you from realizing your full potential.

What You Feel Is What You Are.

The two—thinking and feeling—cannot be separated. When you think about anything, you also experience a feeling in conjunction with that thought. Your thoughts can only become a tangible reality if your mind channels the energy contained within the feelings you experience. Whatever you feel when you think about your dream is exactly what you will obtain in your life.

One of the main reasons why a lot of individuals don't succeed in bringing their goals into reality is because they falsely believe that the Law of Attraction is solely about thinking hard and concentrating on what you want. A lot of people are under the impression that the power of the mind consists in its capacity for thought. They have the misconception that thinking positively is sufficient.

However, despite the fact that they are not the same thing, thinking and feeling are connected. The conscious mind is responsible for mental processes such as thinking and concentrating, whereas the subconscious mind is responsible for feelings. Both the conscious mind and the subconscious mind are comparable to operating a motor vehicle. The conscious mind is like a driver, while the subconscious mind is like the vehicle itself. While the conscious mind steers or drives, the subconscious mind is the one that actually gets you where you need to go. Through thought, we are able to direct our attention. Simply by feeling it, we bring it into manifestation in our lives.

Take this into consideration, okay? Thinking and feeling are two very different things! Different from having a pleasant sensation is having a positive thought! The majority of publications and instructors will merely tell you to have a positive mental attitude toward your goals, but having a positive mental attitude is far more vital. Even if you have optimistic thoughts about your goals, but if you have a pessimistic outlook on them, you will never be successful in achieving them. If your ideas and feelings are not aligned, you will never be successful in getting what you want.

Although having happy thoughts increases the likelihood that you will experience positive feelings, this is not a guarantee. I am aware that you have encountered this situation quite a few times. I have faith that you have ever attempted to accomplish a goal or target. You had the impression that it was impossible to accomplish it, but you remained optimistic and told yourself, "Do not worry. You have the ability to do it! What you believe will end up being the case. If you believe that you are capable of doing something, then you will be. Maintain your positive attitude!!" You continued to experience unpleasant feelings, but you chose to disregard those feelings and instead believe in optimistic thoughts. And would you believe it? The passage of time has brought both months and years, yet you have not yet accomplished it.

A lot of individuals have the mindset that if they think positively, they will feel positively. This is a common misunderstanding. Your feelings and emotions are not susceptible to being manipulated by your thoughts. Your feelings have the power to influence the thoughts that you have. Have you ever experienced anxiety as a result of something that went wrong? You commanded yourself to take a deep breath and reassured yourself that everything would be all right. You tried to think positively, but your emotions were all over the place. You experienced an increase in feelings of anxiety. In addition to that, the predicament was getting even worse.

The act of thinking positively requires more work than repressing or rejecting your feelings would require. This statement was made from the perspective of a therapist, not one of a motivator. Stop thinking about your goal or dream if doing so makes you feel uneasy or horrible about yourself.

The conscious part of one's mind is responsible for thinking, whereas the subconscious part of one's mind is responsible for feeling. The conscious mind is limited in comparison to the power of the subconscious mind. In situations where the conscious mind and the subconscious mind are at odds with one another, the subconscious mind will prevail. When there is a battle between our thoughts and our emotions, our feelings almost always emerge victorious.

The power of positive thought cannot be understated. But in order to tap into its potential, we need to maintain an optimistic attitude. The majority of individuals have the belief that all they need to do is think positively, and everything will work out just great. If we are feeling down, there is no point in trying to think positively. If we are experiencing negative emotions, thinking positively may have the opposite effect on us. Even if you have a positive attitude toward your goals and objectives, if you do not feel good, you will not be able to realize them.

How do you feel about the dream that you had? How do you feel about having achieved success?

Take a few moments to think about a dream, goal, or want you have. You might affirm, "I am confident and believe that I can achieve (your dreams or goals)" It should be done ten times. While you are affirming, pay attention to how you are feeling! Do you experience positive feelings such as passion, enthusiasm, motivation, gratitude, and other pleasant feelings? Or do you experience feelings of unworthiness, lack of confidence, anxiety, resentment, or other undesirable emotions?

You need to address whatever is making you uncomfortable or giving you unpleasant feelings first before moving on. It's the same as being sick when you get an uncomfortable feeling. When you become ill, your body is trying to communicate with you and let you know that something is wrong. You have no choice but to get some rest, take the medicine, or see a medical professional. It will get worse if all you do is think positively and do nothing about it. The same phenomenon happens when you experience discomfort; your subconscious mind is trying to notify you that something is amiss. You can't ignore the uneasy feeling you're having; rather than that, focus on being optimistic.

The Sedona Method is one of the strategies that proves to be useful in overcoming unfavorable feelings. The core of the Sedona Method consists on acknowledging and accepting one's challenging feelings before releasing them. By guiding our subconscious brains, we are able to let go of the unpleasant emotions. Once we are able to let go of our bad feelings, happy feelings are able to flourish.

1. Embrace the sensation that you are experiencing.

If you experience unease while repeating the affirmation, you should make an effort to figure out what feeling it is that you are experiencing. Is it a feeling of inadequacy, worthlessness, lack of confidence, or something else? The more particular you can be, the better! Just allow yourself to feel whatever it is that you are experiencing and focus on feeling the emotion.

You are able to provide a number between 0 and 10. A score of ten indicates that the unfavorable feeling is very powerful. Zero indicates that the unfavorable feeling has been eradicated.

2. Pose the following questions to yourself:
Would it be possible for me to let go of this feeling?
Would I be willing to let go of this feeling?

When would it be appropriate for me to let it go?

3. Keep going until you feel comfortable answering the questions freely.
Repeat the questions from above until you feel comfortable answering them freely. Because the questions are intended for your subconscious mind and not for your conscious mind, there is no need for you to provide a response.

It is important to keep in mind that this is a matter of the heart, not the head. The concentration on the questions, rather than the solutions, is necessary for the success of this strategy. It does not make a difference what responses you provide. Continue to ask yourself the same questions until you no longer feel the unpleasant emotion or until it drops to zero.

The Sedona Method, Ho'oponopono, Resource Therapy, Emotional Freedom Technique, and a great many other practices can all be helpful in overcoming unfavorable feelings, but these are just a few examples. Emotional Freedom Technique is my go-to method. You might find it helpful to read Manifesting Mastery with EFT: The Step-by-Step Guide to Attracting Abundance Using Emotional Freedom Technique, which is the title of my last book.

Your mind will use the feeling that you are experiencing as either energy or fuel in order to bring about the dream that you have. Your mind will use the feeling you are experiencing to bring your notion into physical reality. You are the sum total of your emotions.

Be Specific Regarding Your Goals, And Make Sure The Universe Is Aware Of Them

You have made a good deal of progress thus far toward reducing the amount of stress in your life, centering your attention on the things that truly matter, and become more tranquil. You are almost finished with your journey of manifesting things through tranquillity and peace, and the last thing you need to do is understand the method that will bring you success. In order for the universe to provide you with precisely what you require, it is necessary for you to communicate to it very specifically what it is that you want.

Establish Crystal-Clear Objectives and Maintain Open Communication with the Universe

You have to be one hundred percent certain of what it is that you want before you can expect the ideas that you send out into the universe to assist you in achieving that objective. In order to accomplish this, you will need to compile a list of your long-term objectives as well as a separate list of your short-term objectives. The short-term goals are broken up into smaller chunks of time and lead to the achievement of the long-term goals.

After that, it is necessary for you to practice conscious breathing in order to calm yourself down, and then you should communicate with the cosmos. Repeat to yourself and the universe the primary objective you have set for yourself in order to get started on achieving your goals. Say something like, "I want the universe's help to help me get admission into (college's name.)" if your objective is to enroll in a reputable law school, for instance, and you want to increase your chances of doing so. Say it out loud and make sure to inject a great deal of belief in it because your belief in this proposal is exactly what is going to reinforce it and make it impactful enough to encourage the universe to help you.

Saying it out loud and making sure to inject a great deal of belief in it is the best way to encourage the universe to assist you.

If you do it multiple times throughout the day, you'll quickly find that you're presented with wonderful possibilities that will assist you in achieving the goal you've set for yourself. It is essential that you conduct a thorough analysis of each option if you wish to be in a position to make an intelligent choice.

In addition to carrying out this exercise, you will also need to engage in some type of visualization. The practice of visualization is a strong tactic that brings you that much closer to accomplishing your goal. To put it into practice, all you have to do is see yourself successfully completing your objective. Include a wealth of specifics in this scene, and strive to make it feel as alive as you can. If you engage in this behavior on a consistent basis, you will soon receive assistance in materializing what it is that you want.

If you pay attention to all of the tips and techniques described in this book, you won't need to stick to a packed agenda if you want to do the things you set out to do. Your life will improve in quality and happiness after you have an understanding of and begin to use the principles of manifestation through peace.

Never Give In: "Never Give Up"

The first and most important rule of success is to never, under any circumstances, give up. When we are confronted with challenging circumstances on our path to achievement, we are frequently tempted to give up since doing so is always the choice that presents the least amount of effort. When things go rough, that is the time to work twice as hard instead of giving up; the pursuit of success is not an easy path, and you must be prepared to fail before you can achieve. If you want to be successful, you must be prepared to fail before you can succeed.

When things grow difficult, everyone experiences the emotions of hopelessness and skepticism. No matter how large or little the goals are that you wish to accomplish, you will inevitably confront difficult periods in which your dedication and motivation will be put to the test to an extent that seems unattainable. At this point, self-doubt begins to set in, and you begin to feel as though there is no hope, but it is essential to keep in mind that difficult times are cyclical; they do not remain constant. When you have a reason for the aims and objectives you have set for yourself, giving up should not be an option. If you have a strong belief in what you're trying to accomplish, you'll have the perseverance to get through the obstacles that may otherwise cause you to give up.

If you give in to the urge to give up, you will spend the rest of your life wondering what would have happened if you had kept pushing forward rather than giving in to the desire to give up. If you want to be successful, you need to have the mental fortitude to fight through the toughest challenges and resist the most alluring distractions along the path to achievement. If you give up, you can be certain that you will not achieve the goals that you have set for yourself.

Why it is Important That You Do Not Give Up on Yourself

In a mindset that prioritizes financial success and wealth accumulation, there is no room for giving up.

You have the strength to overcome the urge to give up.

The purpose and goals you've set for yourself are more important than the urge to give up. The amount of effort and labor that you have already put into your path to success is larger than the difficulties that you are currently encountering. The difficulties we face are only transitory. Have faith in yourself, and keep in mind that trying times won't endure forever.

It is entirely in one's head.

Your frame of mind will determine whether you give up or continue to fight for what you believe in. Your mental toughness will determine whether you are successful or unsuccessful in facing challenges and overcoming obstacles.

The road to success is not a simple one.

To put this in perspective for you, achieving success is not a walk in the park. To succeed, you will need to put in a lot of effort and have a lot of patience. Always be ready to deal with any challenges life may bring your way.

It takes time to achieve one's goals.

The road to success requires a lot of hard work and patience. There is no such thing as an overnight success. If you start out on the road to success with the expectation that you will become wealthy overnight, you are setting yourself up for failure and are more likely to give up along the way. Many people have the misconception that successful people arrived at their current position overnight; yet, if you ask them, you will discover that their path to success was littered with failures and setbacks that were only overcome because of their unwavering determination to be successful.

Quitting will become second nature to you.

If you give up even once, you will leave a trail of ambitions and aspirations that are only partially accomplished or completed. It is not difficult at all to develop a pattern of failing, and just like any other habit, failing becomes easier with practice.

How to Prevent Giving Up and Maintain Your Motivation

It is essential to maintain concentration as well as motivation in order to pursue and accomplish one's goals. You need constant dedication to be able to fulfill the goals you have set for yourself if you want to maintain your motivation while you are working toward achieving success. Because there is no easy method to reaching goals that will help us realize our purpose and vision, it takes consistent effort to turn a goal into an accomplishment, which in turn involves a persistent concentration on the task at hand. Having focus can allow you to materialize your objectives, making it much simpler for you to achieve them.

Here are some things you may do to keep your attention on the task at hand and maintain your motivation to reach your goals:

Try to avoid thinking negatively at all costs.

The pursuit of one's goals while harboring negative thoughts is counterproductive. It is important to keep negative ideas at bay and replace them with thoughts of achievement and positive affirmations as much as possible. If all you can do is think negatively, there is no way you will ever be successful at anything. Even in the face of setbacks and defeats, it is important to maintain a positive outlook and celebrate even the little victories.

Be aware that it is normal to experience setbacks.

Nobody anticipates that you will always be successful, and you shouldn't act as if they do. Acknowledge and accept that it is okay to fail, and that it is likely that you will fail a few times while working toward achieving your goals. Your objective ought to be to put up your utmost effort in order to realize your objectives. Focus on the progress you've made and how you can apply what you've learned to achieve success in the future rather than dwelling on the fact that you didn't reach your objective.

Recognize that you alone are accountable for your achievements and success.

There is no room for justifications or pointing fingers; whether you achieve or fall short of your objectives is entirely the result of your own actions. Once you have the epiphany that you alone are responsible for your success or failure, you will never forget the significance of the steps involved in getting there, and you will work harder to guarantee that your objectives are met.

Try not to be too critical of yourself all the time.

If you want to make money and be successful, there is no room for perfection in any of those things. Be your own strongest ally and remind yourself frequently to push yourself in the direction you want to go. Your ability to concentrate and remain motivated will suffer if you are too hard on yourself when you experience failure.

Put the past in the past.

You have either fallen short of achieving one of your milestones or missed a deadline, right? Do not allow this to be a burden that follows you around for the rest of your life and hinder you from moving forward with confidence. There will be obstacles along the way; the important thing is to get back up and keep going. Negative thoughts are encouraged by unpleasant experiences and recollections. It is essential to learn from one's mistakes and to ensure that one does not let the past to dictate the course of one's future.

Keep your mind on the possibilities.

In order to keep your attention on the task at hand, avoid being overly idealistic or ambitious. Keep your focus on what is achievable. Focus on improving the aspects of your life that are within your control while always assessing and reminding yourself of the positive aspects of your character and ability.

Maintaining coherence.

To be consistent means that you must be willing to go the distance, commit and dedicate yourself to taking action over the long term in order to accomplish the goals that you have set for yourself, and keep doing so until you succeed. It indicates that you are able to resist and overcome distractions in order to keep your eyes on the price, and it boils down to the fact that you are repetitive.

Because it educates the brain to engage in the routine that will enable you to reach your goals, consistency requires that you repeat the same habits over and over again until they become second nature. If you want to be consistent, you have to do this. If you do something on a daily basis, your brain will find it much simpler to transform a behavior that you engage in repeatedly into a habit.

Rescue From The Wrath Of Sin

When one needs deliverance from the bondage of sin, then fasting is essential in order to break the power of that sin and keep you safe and free from it. Fasting is also required when one is in need of deliverance from the bondage of another sin. According to the book of Isaiah, 58 verse 6, "Does not the kind of fasting that I have decided to engage in loosen the chains of injustice and untie the cords of the yoke, to set the oppressed free and break every yoke?

The followers of Christ were instructed to fast in order to be able to exorcise a demon from a kid and rescue the youngster from his captivity; Matthew 17:21 states that "howbeit this kind goeth not out but by prayer and fasting."

Jesus enlightened them to the fact that there is a hierarchical structure to the many kinds of deliverance. I have seen numerous instances of that, including one in which the devil was speaking out with a masculine voice from the body of a female. I have also witnessed situations in which this has occurred. It is really terrible, and some of those demons are obstinate and can only be driven out of a person if that person has prepared themselves by prayer and fasting.

When some people in the Bible attempted to drive demons out of their bodies, we saw what the demons did to them.... Eventually, one of the wicked spirits replied them, saying, "Jesus I know, Paul I know about, but who are you?" (Acts 19:15).

The kind of fast that is required in this kind of scenario is a three-day absolute fast, also known as a dry fast, during which time the individual prays to God for more power to cast out devils and abstains from water and food.

PRAYERS Verse N) Then they cried out to the LORD in their despair, and he delivered them from their afflictions... PRAYERS107:6 of the Psalms

PRAYER POINTS 1) In the name of Jesus, may the sin that is rooted in your life and in your home be uprooted completely.

2) In the name of Jesus Christ, may your loads be taken from you immediately, and may you experience the inner peace that only God can give.

Manifesting Calls For Creative Thought And Action.

It's not something new at all. The practice of creative visualization has been around since far before the time that Jesus walked the world. You are, in point of fact, already doing it on a daily basis by merely making use of your imagination. It is a method in which you harness the inherent power of your own ideas in order to form a distinct mental image of anything that you desire. And it's a powerful strategy to employ if you want to bring a wish into reality.

It may be the hot new romantic interest that you've been hoping will be dropped into your life at just the right moment.

The riches that can be enjoyed by both your children and the offspring of your children in the future.

sculpted abdominal muscles that you can't help but look at whenever you walk by a mirror when you're at the gym.

The power of your thoughts is where you should begin to harness the potential to experience the hot side of existence.

Visualization exercises are designed to assist you in concentrating on your objectives and establishing a connection with your higher self and your life's work. Your alignment with the natural laws that govern the universe will improve as a result of this. You will be able to learn how to use those ideas in a way that is both more mindful and appealing as a result of doing so.

When fully comprehended, creative vision has the power to bring into reality anything a person can dream about. It is also a wonderful way to visualize your own life as being as beautiful as the home of your favorite influencer on Instagram.

As you develop the practice of creative vision into a habit and learn to place your faith in the outcomes that it is capable of producing, you will realize that it becomes an indispensable component of your way of thinking. It develops into a constant state of awareness in which you are aware that you are the one responsible for creating your existence.

The end goal of practicing creative visualization is to make each and every moment of our lives the best and most rewarding versions of those moments that we can possibly envision.

A Workout That Involves Visualization

Remembering to make frequent use of creative imagery is the single most crucial thing to keep in mind. I strongly suggest that you engage in imaginative visualisation on a daily basis, at the very least once. Make sure to incorporate it into your daily meditation practice, both when you first get up in the morning and when you get ready for bed at night. Always begin your meditation by entering a state of profound relaxation, and then proceed to practice imagery and affirmations. There will be further discussion on these issues in Chapters 9 and 11.

An illustration of what it means to envision can be found here. Take some time to read through this exercise, and pay attention to what comes easily to you:

Find a comfortable position in which you can sit up straight with your hands supported by your thighs. Put your eyes out and take a few deep breaths. Take a few full breaths in here. Take note of how your tummy is expanding as a result of your lungs taking in breath, and maintain this position for a few seconds. Next, let your breath out slowly. As you let out your breath, picture the tension in your body being released and carried away by the wind.

Feeling comfortable, serene, and at ease throughout your entire body. Observe how your body, including your arms and legs, is beginning to relax. The tension in your head, neck, chest, arms, and back is beginning to melt away as a wave of calm travels down through your legs and reaches your feet.

Just for a moment, picture yourself making your way towards a serene, picture-perfect beach with white sand. You set out on foot and begin walking along the shoreline, which goes on for as far as the eye can see.

You can feel the sun's warmth creeping across your face as it begins to rise. You can feel the warmth of the sand on your feet as you stroll across it. At the same time, a gentle breeze from the ocean is gently brushing over your skin.

You turn your attention to the azure waters of the ocean and notice the white peaks of the waves as they approach the coastline. You stop what you're doing to gaze at the breathtaking sea.

You relax as you take in the soothing sound of the waves breaking gently on the coast. The waves are reaching a point where they are washing up onto the white sandy beach and then retreating back to the ocean. Clearing the slate and circling around. Clearing the slate and circling around.

You take another deep breath in and smell the freshness of the air that has a hint of saltiness to it. You give yourself permission to feel appreciative for the calming effect that the ocean breeze has on you.

As you amble along the shore in a relaxed manner, you come across a comfortable beach chair buried in the sand. You settle into the chair beside the water and take a few deep breaths as you do so. You take pleasure in the comfortable warmth of the sun, the refreshing chill of the breeze, and the relaxing lull of the waves.

Now, think back to something enjoyable that happened to you during the past few days, particularly something that involved positive bodily feelings such as eating a nice meal, getting a massage, or making love. Recall the event in as much detail as you can and take pleasure in experiencing those gratifying sensations once more.

As you continue to lay there in your beach chair, you allow yourself to sink more and further into the plush chair, and you start to feel increasingly peaceful.

You experience a complete state of calmness. Your stress has completely dissipated at this point.

When you are ready, make a gradual transition back into your regular routine after your trip. Bring your focus back to the room in a calm and steady manner while you are still experiencing a peaceful and comfortable state. Maintain that state of calm in both your mind and body as you bring yourself back to the here and now. You'll feel much better once you rub your eyes, stretch, and open your eyes.

Nevertheless, in order to better "visualize" the situation, you conjured up this image in your head. This is an excellent activity to perform if you feel the urge to press the reset button. You'll discover, through repeated use, how tremendously useful it is.

Get in touch with the Badass that resides within you.

Connecting with your higher power, often known as the badass that resides within you, is one of the most essential elements in the visualization process. Your higher power is the boundless wellspring of love, wisdom, and vitality that is contained inside the cosmos.

Regardless matter what you believe, the majority of people hold the concept that there is some sort of greater force. Recognizing that there is a higher power that we may turn to for assistance when we are in need makes us feel more supported. In addition to this, it helps us get back in touch with our purpose and gives us the confidence to pursue our goals with vigor.

Establishing a connection with your higher power is analogous to communicating with the version of the Jedi master Yoda that is deep within you. As soon as you do so, you will have a profound sense of clarity regarding your power, love, and wisdom. You will have a revitalized feeling of self-assurance once you realize that you have the power to create the experiences that are most meaningful to you throughout your life.

During your meditations, you may experience powerful emotions, such as the sensation that you are "on top of the world" or that you are "able to move mountains." It is possible that you will even feel a warm radiant glow go through your body at this time. These are signs that you are establishing a connection with your divine source or higher power.

There are two distinct ways to connect with the higher power in your life. You can either choose to be Receptive or Active in the situation.

When you access your intuitive mind and seek your higher power (or the Yoda that is within you) for direction, you are said to be "being receptive." You are able to complete this task while meditating in peace. Allow the answers to come to you by opening up your spirit and waiting for them.

You are engaging in active living when you acknowledge that you are a co-creator of your life. You might consider the universe to be your co-signer for the things you want to happen in your life. You can accomplish this by visualizing and affirming that you have already accomplished what you set out to do.

Your ability to be guided by your higher power during meditation increases when you are both receptive and active during the practice. You will then create the greatest and most beautiful version of your life based on the choices you make based on the instruction you receive.

Why Positive Thinking Is Effective

There has been a significant amount of scientific investigation done to demonstrate that affirmations are effective. If you don't trust me, you may verify this information for yourself. You can learn about what science, particularly psychology and neuroscience, has to say regarding the efficacy of affirmations with just a fast search on Google. You will discover ample resources to support your investigation.

Because of how beneficial they are, a significant number of psychologists and therapists consistently suggest them to the patients in their care.

But why do affirmations have such an effect?

They are successful for one very straightforward reason: the human mind is unable to differentiate between what is real and what is not real. Obviously, one can draw both positive and bad conclusions from this. Because of this, you might laugh at a funny show, become furious when something horrible occurs to your favorite character on TV, or even cry after watching a movie or TV show. Your thinking does not reflect the fact that all of those are works of fiction, which you are aware of. This is the reason why you find yourself sobbing, laughing, and becoming upset over imaginary events and characters.

Affirmations play a role in this process because they allow you to exploit a potential weakness in your thinking that may be turned to your benefit.

By the way, a good number of people already do this. Have you ever come across a person who harbors a wide variety of unfavorable views about themselves? those who are always criticizing others, whether it be by saying they are ugly, obese, incompetent, or foolish, are known as "people who say all sorts of negative things." Each and every one of those terrible sayings is an affirmation (clearly a negative one), and the more often they are repeated, the more powerful those beliefs become. The wonderful thing is, though, that it also works in the opposite direction, and that is where the affirmations included in this guide come into play.

The fact of the matter is that each one of us has mental scripts that operate in the background. One of the many benefits of using positive affirmations is that they allow you to exert control over the scripts that are executed in the background, which refers to your subconscious mind.

When you take control of the scripts that your subconscious mind runs, you give yourself the ability to actively participate in determining the path that your life takes as well as the outcomes that you experience.

Affirmations of a positive nature have a tremendous amount of power. There is a good reason why they have been advocated by the most intelligent individuals throughout history and have been practiced by the most knowledgeable people throughout history for hundreds of years. Simply look up the scriptures in the Bible, the teachings of Buddha, or any other religious or spiritual books for that matter, and you will see exactly what I am referring to.

Affirmations are effective and have the potential to make a significant difference in your life for the better. In order to assist you in accomplishing this goal, I have compiled thirty extremely potent affirmations that will assist you in taking charge of both your life and your future. These are affirmations that I formulated after testing them out in my own life for a number of years, and the ones listed here are the thirty that I found to be the most effective. They are designed to target and enhance several crucial aspects of your life, and each and every one of them packs quite a bit of a punch in terms of their effectiveness.

Getting started must fill you with a lot of eager anticipation, doesn't it?

So, let's just dive right in, shall we?

The Hidden Truth Behind The Principle Of Attraction

Always keep in mind that like attracts like, and that all that stands between you and the fulfillment of your dreams is the correct energy and alignment on your part.

You materialize what you focus on the most, so be careful what you think about. "Thoughts become Things" is a proverb that really rings true. Therefore, you should keep an eye on both your sensations and your thoughts. If you have a positive mood, it indicates that you are thinking positive ideas, which in turn means you are attracting positive experiences and the things you want in life. In addition to this, you are in harmony with the desires that are already materializing for you. If you're feeling down, it's a sign that your thoughts are negative and that you're attracting upsetting occurrences through your thoughts. Additionally, you are not in harmony with the desires that you wish to bring into manifestation.

Therefore, whatever it is that you seek, whether it is an Ultimate Lover, a Career, or Financial Abundance, etc., make sure that you experience it in every level of your being. Put all of your attention on what it is that you want, rather than on the things that you are afraid of or the things that you don't want to happen.

The principle of attraction does neither favor or disfavor anyone. It never stops operating and delivering to you the thoughts that predominate as well as whichever energy or vibration you are experiencing at any given moment. This is a process that never ends.

Whatever it is that you put your passionate attention on is what speeds up the process of its manifestation. No matter how good or how horrible it is.

Do not let yourself get all up if you find that you are having negative thoughts or thoughts that originate from the default mode or the automatic thinking process of the past.

The power of a positive Positive thought is one hundred times more than the strength of a negative idea.

I know it won't sit well with you to hear this, but everything that's bothering you right now or causing you stress was drawn to you, either unknowingly or deliberately (by default). I'm sorry to be the bearer of bad news, but that's the truth. Your life is an expression of your thoughts and feelings. You are responsible for the creation of your own cosmos as you progress. Therefore, in order to become a conscious maker of your own life, you must have control over your ideas and feelings.

2

Make use of the Creative Process in order to bring about whatever it is that you wish.

The first step is to beg or summon the universe for what it is you need and want. Begin by keeping a journal of thankfulness in which you continue to write, "I am so happy and grateful now that......." (Talk about whatever you want as though you already have it and are expressing gratitude for it right now.) Second, have trust that cannot be shaken, and believe! Affirm to yourself every time you have a negative idea or worry purge out owing to the fact that there are no physical indicators of manifestation on the surface level with "I know it (desired outcome) is on its way."

Third, maintain the momentum of your faith by practicing gratitude, and be ready and in alignment to receive what it is that you want. Find out what you need in order to create the impression that you already have it right now.

There are also occasions when actions are essential, particularly if the chance presents itself or if you have a hunch that you ought to take a move.

The Law of Attraction teaches that there is a powerful method that may be used to create your wishes, and its name is Visualization. Always keep in mind that the saying goes, "when you visualize, you materialize." When you have visited a location in your head, your physical self will be able to replicate that experience. Put yourself in the position of the sensation. Instead of treating this as a chore or obligation, do it whenever you have the urge or are in a good mood.

In conclusion, it is not our duty to figure out the "How" component; rather, the "How" will be figured out as a result of our dedication and our faith in the "What." The universe is in charge of answering the question "how"! The cosmos is aware of the means that are the simplest, most expedient, and most congruent with your goals in order to bring them into manifestation.

Gratitude-Centered Mentality

If you want to live the life of your dreams, you have to learn to be grateful for all you already have in your life. Being grateful for the things you already possess is a great way to bring additional good fortune into your life. Being grateful for the things you already possess will make you feel good, and when you feel good, you will radiate positive energy, which will speed up the process of the things you want to manifest coming into your life.

The following is a list of suggestions that will assist you in preserving an attitude of gratitude:

1. Reflect on the many blessings that have been bestowed upon you. The majority of people spend a significant amount of time griping about things that they do not desire. As a direct consequence of this, they are producing a greater quantity of that. Therefore, if you want to have even more blessings in

your life, you need to learn how to count the ones you already have. You have a lot to be thankful for; the following are just a few examples:

You owe your parents your gratitude for raising you. They are the ones who gave you life, and even though you may find them bothersome at times, especially if they interfere with your life, they only want the best for you because they are the ones who gave you life.

You should be glad for your job because it enables you to pay the bills, but that is not the only reason.

You should express gratitude for all of the tangible things you own. The reality is that you are wealthier than the vast majority of people in the world if you own a home, drive a car, and are able to eat at least three times per day.

Always remember to be grateful for your friends because no matter what, they will be there for you.

Always remember to count your blessings, especially the ones that come in the form of lessons learned the hard way.

2. Keep a thankfulness diary in which you document the people and experiences for which you are thankful. By doing this, you will be reminded that you have more blessings than you give yourself credit for. Every day, make it a point to list at least ten things for which you are thankful.

3. Show appreciation to the folks who have been kind to you by expressing your gratitude to them. Make it a routine to always offer your gratitude. "Thank you" In addition, make it a routine to send even the simplest of thank-you notes to those who have been helpful to you. They will be encouraged to continue doing pleasant things if you thank them in a sincere manner.

The principle of attraction and its laws

Have you ever had one of those days where everything seems to go your way, from discovering money in unexpected places to getting a significant discount on something you've wanted for a long time to obtaining a new employment opportunity?

When something like this occurs, we automatically think that it is our turn or that we are winning. It would appear that these opportunities are coming in an unpredictable manner and are beyond our ability to regulate them.

On the other hand, those times when you're having a "lucky" or "hot streak" are anything but random. The principle of attraction is proving to be successful for us right now.

The law of attraction refers to what exactly?

This law asserts that our ideas possess the capacity to bring into our life everything and everything that our hearts desire. We have the ability to control the outcomes of the events and situations that take place in our life.

It is predicated on the idea that both positive and negative vibrations make up the cosmos, and that we attract everything that vibrates at the same frequency as our thoughts. This idea forms the basis of the law of attraction.

Have you ever declared, "This isn't your day," only to have a string of unfortunate events follow your proclamation? When you tell yourself things like "today is not my day," you reflect who you are to other people and attract experiences that are consistent with what you believe.

On the other hand, if you think you have a good run of luck, you will approach challenges with a more optimistic attitude. This will allow you to find solutions to problems more quickly, connect more effectively with the people around you, and thus gain access to greater prospects. Your stance will be strengthened as a result of this. who is undeniably having a good run right now?

A constructive attitude on life will drive you to reach your goals since it will ensure that you are willing to do so and that you have faith in your own talents. It will also put you in contact with people and circumstances that will be of assistance to you.

What Exactly Does "Intentional Living" Entail?

When you are able to demonstrate that you are a person of great character, it is because you have learned to live consciously. The manner in which we live our life and the decisions that we make are reflections of who we are. We make choices about how we are going to behave, what we are going to do, and what you are going to think about every morning when we start our day, and we continue to make those choices throughout the day. This is your very first chance to show others that you have integrity and decency, so make the most of it! Your actions will determine the kinds of goals and objectives that you are able to successfully achieve.

Your disposition and mindset are direct reflections of the concepts that are most prevalent in your head. Throughout the course of the day, you will accept responsibility for those thoughts. Beginning your adventure into the world of intentional living with these steps is the recommended way to get started.

At other instances, you will have to coerce yourself to stop thinking about one specific and instead focus your attention on something else in order to divert your attention. It makes no difference what it is, as long as it is something that is beneficial to your health and makes you happy whenever you think about it.

You were given this life to fulfill a specific mission. If you want success and happiness in life, you won't find either by aimlessly drifting through it without a purpose—that is, unless your idea of happiness is to be slothful and unproductive. You do not have to live that way, despite the fact that there may be a large number of individuals who do live that way. You have already made the decision to live a life that is purposeful, one that will bring you personal success and a great deal of happiness for the rest of your life because you are reading this book, which means that you have chosen to live the antithesis of what I just described.

What will bring you the most success and happiness, as well as the best method to spend your life so that you can achieve those goals, ought to be the primary focus of your life. You are going to need to use your imagination. By this, we mean that your life is not going to be a clear route to success simply because you have determined that it is going to be, and you will need to do some creative thinking in order to change things and circumstances so that they are more favorable to you. You cannot anticipate that your roadmap will be completely free of flaws. There may likely be occasions when the many commitments and tasks that you have placed on your agenda cause you to feel overwhelmed. You need to make the effort to shift your ideas to those of motivation and dedication to the activities you engage in, ensuring that each of these activities contributes to your forward movement rather than backward movement. You are going to run across problems, but you should never go in the wrong direction. Try not to turn around. Maintain your optimism and trust as you look to the future.

In order to live a life guided by purpose, you must first examine your life as it stands at the outset of your transition. You have a responsibility to be aware of the reasons behind the things you do, and vice versa. Every day, the decisions we make are influenced by our perceptions of what may or may not be in our best interests. It is expected of us to steer clear of activities that do not contribute to our progress and welfare, while we should make every effort to advance in the directions that do.

It is quite simple to become preoccupied with what other people are doing. When you know that other people are living their lives in the same way, it makes it simpler for you to do the same. However, it's possible that what's best for them isn't what's best for you at this point in your life. You need to think about things from your own perspective while also taking into account how they will impact the people and relationships in your life, particularly your immediate family. If you are married, your decisions should take into account both your partner and their health and happiness. If you have children, it is imperative that you include their needs and considerations in the calculation.

In the end, the benefits of your intentional living should not just accrue to you but also to those closest to you, including your family and loved ones.

You won't simply be "going through the motions" in this situation. You are not going to make significant adjustments to your way of life in order to conform to what everyone else is doing. It's possible that you'll make decisions that are generally accepted, but you'll be aware of the reasons behind them and how they'll help you in the long run.

Because you start to think about how all of your decisions will impact the world around you, intentional living forces you to confront the "why" question. You will choose the ideal route for you by examining what you are already doing and what needs to change in order to live your life with the aim of achieving great success and happiness. The possibilities will be presented to you, and you will select the best route from among them.

When our thoughts are focused on good change and you set about taking the appropriate actions, it is practically a guarantee that you will arrive at your target. When our thoughts are focused on positive change and we take the proper measures. You can't start walking in a certain route and expect to never arrive at your destination. As long as you maintain forward momentum, you will eventually reach your destination. Your responses and decisions will influence how "easy" and "quickly" you arrive to your destination.

You have to accept the fact that you will not always make the ideal decisions when you are moving forward. As you go, you will discover that there will be times when you deviate from the path. As time goes on, you will also come to the realization that a choice you have already made or a path you are now pursuing will inevitably require reevaluation and modification. Your life will be affected in some way by the choices made by other people. They could be constructive or destructive. In either case, you will need to find a means to maneuver around those selections in order to guarantee that you remain on the course that leads to your individual level of success. You can't allow yourself to be sidetracked or derailed by the conduct of other people. It won't be simple, but it won't be impossible, either.

If you are committed to living intentionally, it won't matter what other people throw at you because you will be on your own road, living the life you want to live, regardless of what happens.

This can bring to mind the practice of making resolutions for the new year. Every time a new year begins, you and a lot of other people consider the "resolutions" that you have on the things you want to accomplish in your life. On the other hand, living consciously does not consist of establishing resolutions that are so readily abandoned. Even when you have accomplished your long-term objectives, you should continue to wake up every morning and recommit to these resolutions by carrying them out in the next day.

Think of anything that you would like to occur in the future. It could be something insignificant, like receiving a text message from a certain person, or it could be something significant, like becoming a famous model or actor. After you've chosen the circumstance you wish to bring into existence, you should begin to consider in terms of 3, 6, and 9 after that. One theory suggests that you should begin the manifestation process three times in the morning, then increase the number of times you do it during the day, and end with nine times in the evening.

Numerology and the principle of attraction are both incorporated into the 369 approach, as Zalucky explains.

The following is an explanation of the meaning behind each successive number in the sequence:

- The number three is symbolic of our relationship to the source, or the universe, as well as our capacity for creative self-expression

- The number six is symbolic of our inner fortitude and harmony. - The number nine is symbolic of our inner rebirth (in the sense of letting go of that which no longer serves us and turning into the person we are becoming) (Regan, 2021).

When using this method to bring things into existence, there are a few key things you need to keep in mind at all times:

- THANKFULNESS

The attitude of gratitude is a powerful tool for manifesting because it changes our frame of mind and gives us a sense of plenty. You ought to express gratitude not only for what you have right now but also for the things you have brought into existence. It is a representation of your confidence in the universe when you express gratitude for something that does not yet exist in your physical existence. You are grateful because you are certain that it will be delivered to you regardless of the circumstances. It removes any feeling of uncertainty or worry in relation to your manifestations. To gain an understanding that you are well-provided for, protected, and have plenty of, you need do nothing more than concentrate on the things in your life for which you are grateful.

- THINK ABOUT IT

It is essential to keep in mind that the primary concern relates to what you will get and not what you might acquire in the future. You are required to think of your manifestation as having already taken place in order to adhere to the principles of the Law of Attraction. First, while you are writing, assume that you already have whatever it is that you are trying to bring into existence. Permit yourself to take it in as a real possibility. It is very normal for your thoughts to stray; all you need to do is bring it back to the core. Feelings about the manifestation you've been working on coming to completion should be experienced and emphasized. You have to get your energy and vibration on the same level as the reality you want to create in order to make it happen.

- BE SURE OF IT

In addition to this, it is essential to pay close attention to the way in which you phrase your written affirmation. Create your affirmation as if you already possessed the object you're trying to manifest, and include some of the feelings you have about it, too. If you want to attract a promotion, you could write something like, "I'm so happy and inspired by this promotion I got at work, and it's great to be pushed and recognized for all of my hard work." This will help you bring your intention into reality. This promotion is just what I need to bring out my best self. Writing out your goals and aspirations, given how clear they are to you, is something you should absolutely do, in my opinion. If writing isn't your thing, you can always just say your manifestation out loud three times in the morning, six times in the afternoon, and nine times before bed. Even better, blend the two into one.

Bringing My Wellness Into Manifestation

As I reflected on what I had accomplished in the past month since beginning the course, I began to scribble down the points and make a comparison of my accomplishments to each wish. As I did this, I was able to see that I had already materialized quite a bit. A new form of expression that has recently gained popularity is keeping a gratitude notebook. It's become common knowledge that drinking a glass of warm water with honey in it can leave your skin radiant and clear. Obviously, this trip has been life-changing for me in many ways; for example, although I was aware that certain colors existed, I had no idea that they could be so stunning until now.

Having a healthy body weight was, among many other things, one of the most popular desires.

In an effort to take responsibility for my health, I began the third day of the course by going for brisk walks. But with time, I got into the habit of walking a distance of 2.5 kilometers every day, simply so I could take in the vibrant colors of the rising sun set against the backdrop of the highway while listening to beautiful music and having only myself for company. Even before the sun reached its zenith, I was content with my identity as Sonia. A young woman who, without regard for who might be watching, sings loudly in public while listening to her headphones at full volume. A young woman who, in the early morning hours of winter, uses early morning dew drops to sketch colorful clouds against the street lights. A girl who greeted the children who were leaving for school in the morning with a frown on her face and a wave to let them know that although she felt sad for them, she was actually blessing them on the inside. A young woman who witnessed the color of the feathers on birds' wings transform from silver to gold as the dawning sun reflected off of them. A girl just now handed five rupees to an unrelated girl youngster after observing the child buy a packet of glucose biscuits at 6:20 in the morning. A young woman who began her life with the goal of finding ways to put smiles on the faces of complete strangers in order to convince them that the world is a lovely place. A young woman who began her life as Sonia did, long before she assumed the roles of mother, wife, daughter in law, working professional, or any of the other labels that are automatically bestowed upon people when the rest of the world awakens.

I was the young woman who, every day from 4:30 am until 7:00 am, was able to cross the border with as much liberty as the air itself.

It's possible that I've lost between 100 and 150 grams in a few different places around my body. But what I did gain was endurance, a healthy posture, and happy hormones first thing in the morning. I began this trip by walking briskly; however, as time has gone on, my speed has risen, and it has reached a point where I am now able to run every day!!

My back problems were made much worse by the fact that I worked at a desk. On the other hand, due to the movement in my pelvic body caused by walking, I started generating muscular tension in my upper body, particularly in my shoulder, spine, and upper back. This was caused by the movement in my pelvic body. I had no choice but to perform crunches, Halasana, also known as plough stance, bridge pose, and a few more poses here and there in order to relieve the stress in my muscles. My current fitness routine consists of walking, running, three sets of crunches (15*1), two sets of Halasana or plough pose (10*1), two sets of bridge pose (15*1), and five minutes of my most favorite shavasana stance. I exercise for a total of 45 minutes each and every day. My years-long backache has suddenly vanished, and I have the distinct impression that my back is considerably stronger today.

I went from being a girl who refused to follow any exercise routine because she always thought she never had enough time to becoming a woman who was a prisoner of her own mindset and gave in to the household responsibilities even before they began. I also went from being a woman who always waited for the so-called right time or what you could call free time (this never came, because liabilities never end once you are married), and who was a person who succumbed to the responsibilities even before they began. And this coming from a young lady who puts the requirements of others above her own requirements at all times. I went from being a girl who always believed that this was life and that the only way I would have time for me was when I retired to becoming a woman who takes full responsibility for her life.

I may not have manifested my desired weight of 55 kilograms (down from 62 kilograms), but I have manifested a complete resolution of my concerns with stamina, back discomfort, and other posture problems, which ranged from zero to one hundred percent. And without spending a single dime on a membership to a gym, yoga studio, or any other type of fitness facility, I was able to bring into existence a wholesome morning routine, increased confidence, and a physically fit body.

A Simulated Scenario

But hold on, what feelings are it that you're supposed to have? How do you tell if you're heading in the right direction? I would recommend that, if you are completely new to the practice of scripting for manifestation, you write an actual letter to someone you know, with the aim of mailing that letter. Find a time in your life when you felt an overwhelming sense of thankfulness for something. It may be the day you graduated from high school, the day you got your first job, the day you got your first automobile, your first pet, or the birth of your first kid. In accordance with the TSAR Method, the following actions are suggested:

1) Make sure the letter is addressed to someone.
2) Think back to that particular day.
3) Try to remember as many specifics as you can; activate all of your senses; for example, how did the interior of your car smell? What kind of car was it, and what color was it? How did the seats fit into your body? Who was the one to hand it to you? How did you feel during your very first trip behind the wheel?
4) Dig deep into the feelings that the day brought, and ask yourself whether you were shocked. Are you awed and filled with pride?

After you've finished, go back and read it again. Do you find yourself overcome with feelings of joy and gratitude? If that's the case, you've basically figured out what scripting is all about. Employing the same method, paying the same amount of attention to detail, and checking to see if rereading your letter provokes the same emotional response each time are all necessary steps in the process of using scripting to manifest future results.

Keep the Faith

After you have completed the first step of visualizing your dream or the experiences, things, and people that you want to bring into your life, the next step is to give up control of the process and put your faith in the universe. There are some people who have tried to manifest their aspirations through daily visualization, but their goals have not been realized in the real world. This is due to the fact that they have deeply ingrained unfavorable thoughts and beliefs that are buried deep within their subconscious mind.

To put this into perspective for you, before you can even begin to think about making your goals come true, you need to make some changes to the way you think. You have to have faith in order to succeed. You have to have the mentality that you are deserving of the blessing in order to get it. To have financial success, you must first convince yourself that you are deserving of it. You have to convince yourself that you are worthy of finding someone who truly loves you. You have to convince yourself that you are capable of accomplishing what you set out to do.

The power of faith is something that a great number of spiritual mystics have preached. Do not allow yourself to have any misgivings. When things have not yet presented themselves, you should not become disheartened or doubtful. You only need to continue to have trust in yourself and believe that your dreams will come true in their entirety in order to achieve success.

Get moving on it!
The law of manifestation is a fantastic and amazing principle, but just because it exists does not imply that you are excused from taking any effort toward achieving your goals. Opportunities that will assist you in realizing your dreams

are typically what you may expect to receive as a gift from the universe. For example, if you have always imagined driving a flashy sports vehicle, the universe will present you with additional opportunities to work on so that you can save up enough money to buy that car or perhaps your dream house. But the good news is that if you have an empowering belief and you focus your thoughts on the things that you want, you are more likely to take action and adopt certain behaviors that are necessary in order to achieve those things. This is the good news. The actions you take are inspired by your subconscious mind.

It is essential to keep an eye out for and make the most of chances as soon as they become available to you. It is essential to take prompt action in order to ensure that your goals and desires will be realized.

If you want a career in law, you should apply for the scholarship that was offered to you by the universe and enroll in law school. Obtaining a passport is essential if you wish to go anywhere in the globe. Start chatting to real estate professionals as soon as possible if you want to find your ideal home. Once you have made up your mind about anything, other possibilities and people will continue to present themselves to you.

Keep an attitude of thankfulness at all times.
There is an old proverb that asserts, "A poor attitude is the only disability in life." Being grateful for what one already possesses is an essential component in bringing into one's life more of the things that a person wishes for and yearns for. Take note of all the countless benefits that have already been bestowed upon you.

Be thankful that you have a job, that you have a place to live, that you have a family that loves you, and that there is food on the table. You should be thankful for the money that is already in your bank account as well as the education that you have received. Always remember to be thankful for the natural abilities and qualities that you possess. Always remember to be thankful for the beautiful individuals you have in your life.

A grateful heart is a joyful heart; there is no doubt about it. When you have an attitude of gratitude, you release a positive energy that spreads throughout the universe.

Take some time out of each day to reflect on the things in your life for which you are thankful, no matter how big or how tiny they may be. This will help you develop the habit of thankfulness. It's as easy as being thankful that I have a computer that works or that I have a puppy that's so kind and affectionate. I'm grateful for both of those things.

Keeping a "Gratitude Notebook" is one strategy that has been shown to be beneficial in generating positive vibrations and in assisting individuals in the process of manifesting their hopes, aspirations, and desires. When you wake up in the morning, make it a habit to sit down and jot down a few things for which you are thankful. Always keep doing this. You may also perform this action just before going to bed at night. When you get to the end of the week and read the things that you have written over the course of the past seven days, you will come to the realization that you are genuinely blessed.

Being appreciative for the things that you already have is one of the ways that spiritual gurus have taught their followers to materialize what it is that they want in their lives. Expressing gratitude and appreciation both brings additional gifts into one's life and speeds up the process of manifesting those blessings. Additionally, individuals are typically drawn to a person who exudes positivity, gratitude, and appreciation.

Do not forget to have feelings of gratitude once you have attained the things that you have always desired. Keep in mind the importance of gratitude. Keep in mind how much love and joy there is.

When we direct our thoughts and feelings toward positive things, we set ourselves up to attract more positive experiences and outcomes. It is high time that we cut back on the amount of attention that we devote to our challenges, issues, and fears. It is about time that we concentrate on finding answers, coming up with ideas, and putting all of our effort into making our aspirations come true.

In conclusion, keep in mind the importance of having fun and simply going with the flow. It will be much simpler for you to bring your goals and aspirations into reality if you are experiencing joy and laughter in your life.

Mastering The Art Of Acquiring That Which One Desires

You are most likely not familiar with a level of mindfulness that is available to you but that you can practice. It broadens outwards and ascends above the standard degree of consciousness that you are most typically accustomed to experiencing. At this more elevated level of presence, which you are free to access at any time, the fulfillment of wishes is not merely a possibility; rather, it is a given. At this point, it will be much easier for you to get all of your needs met, including the most obscure ones. You can become the person you were always meant to be by making use of your creative energy, developing the skill of accepting the feeling that your desires have been fulfilled, and resolutely refusing to let any evidence from the outside world divert you from your expectations. If you do these things, you will discover that you have the ability to become the person you were always meant to be as a result of the wisdom of your spiritual mindfulness. What happens next is simply the planning stage for entering that realm, in which you have a significantly greater amount of control over what comes into your life than you could have expected.

Have faith in the fact that you are an eternal spiritual being. Experiencing Something Human For a Brief Moment

Took up the role of an observer of your internal monologue

Free Your Imagination from the Limits Placed Upon It by the Present Situations

Imagine That Your Wish Is Already Granted to You

Have faith in the divine power that is uniquely yours.

Maintain your autonomy with regard to the approval of other individuals.

Rebuild Who You Are, Practice Patience, and Get Rid of Your Doubts

Prepare Yourself to Deal with the Emotion of Having Your Wish Granted

Consider how natural it seems to you for your dream to come true.

Formulate your goals as statements that are already a given.

Choose Your Own Adventure with Love.

Realize that what you already own is sufficient for your needs.

Becoming Even More of the Person That You Already Are

Our potential to transform the life of our thoughts into a form that has not been seen before is the source of our creative power. The end result is called manifestation. You can figure out how to make everything you want happen in your life by beginning with a single objective at a time. Think of yourself as a piece of God's plan that is being carried out in the world, similar to how a wave is a part of the ocean that is being carried out by the ocean. This naturalistic theory will help you develop the kind of trust that is necessary to draw into yourself everything that has a spot reserved for you in the cosmos. In the event that you do not appear to have faith in yourself as an extension of God, you will not be able to gain it or even come close to demonstrating that you have it.

The act of manifesting therefore becomes a question of performing the work necessary to bring another aspect of yourself into structure. You are not producing anything from the materials provided. You are in the process of learning how to adapt yourself to a portion of your being that your faculties have not been aware they might activate. When you have a solid understanding of who you are at your core, you are well on your way to becoming a co-creator of your entire world. You will be able to handle the challenges you face in life and take an active role in the creative process when you have this level of insight. You end up becoming someone who is more manifest. This can give the impression that the "Ask, and you might get" interpretation of the petition that you were probably given with is incorrect. Even if it may feel novel at the time, it is vitally necessary that you acknowledge your own Divine role in the fulfillment of your deepest, most profound yearnings to be adjusted, both for yourself and for other people in the world.

Printed in the USA
CPSIA information can be obtained
at www.ICGtesting.com
LVHW010012100923
757267LV00010B/906